LOOKING AT PAINTINGS

Flowers

The White Heron, 1918–20
Joseph Stella, American (1877–1946)

LOOKING AT PAINTINGS

Flowers

Peggy Roalf

Series Editor
Jacques Lowe

Design
Joseph Guglietti and Steve Kalalian

Hyperion Books for Children
New York

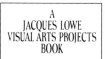

A
JACQUES LOWE
VISUAL ARTS PROJECTS
BOOK

Text © 1993 by Jacques Lowe Visual Arts Projects Inc.

A Jacques Lowe Visual Arts Projects Book

Printed in Italy

FIRST EDITION

1   3   5   7   9   10   8   6   4   2

Library of Congress Catalog Number: 92-72015

ISBN 1-56282-358-2 (trade)/1-56292-359-0 (lib. bdg.)

Original design concept by Amy Hill

Contents

To Barbara and Bob Kreminski, with love

Introduction

LOOKING AT PAINTINGS is a series of books about understanding how great artists see when they paint. Painters have been fascinated by flowers since ancient times. However, it was not until the sixteenth century, when extraordinary new flowers were brought to Europe from the New World and the Far East, that flowers became a major subject in Western art. In *Spring*, a symbolic portrait formed of interwoven blossoms and leaves, Giuseppe Arcimboldo expresses nature's importance in the tapestry of life. One hundred years later, the Dutch painter Abraham Mignon depicted the eternal cycle of birth, growth, death, and rebirth in the intimate woodland scene *Flowers, Animals, and Insects*.

Western painters discovered the arts of the Far East in the middle of the nineteenth century, when Japan opened its doors to trade. Paintings such as Yamamoto Baiitsu's *Egret and Mallow Plants* show a different way of depicting objects in space. The beauty and harmony of Japanese painting profoundly influenced artists such as John La Farge in *Wild Roses and Irises*, Vincent van Gogh in *Sunflowers*, and Claude Monet in *Blue Water Lilies*.

Many twentieth-century painters have affirmed their cultural values and spiritual beliefs through flower paintings. Diego Rivera portrayed an Aztec farm woman to celebrate his Mexican heritage in *The Flower Vendor*. Georgia O'Keeffe enlarged the fragile petals of a sweet pea to express the importance of nature in her life. The enormous rose in René Magritte's *The Wrestlers' Tomb* invites us to use our dreams to understand reality.

Great artists have painted flowers to convey their love of beauty, their spirituality, and their delight in fantasy. Whether you look at a formal garden, a meadow, or your own backyard, you can find inspiration in flowers when you see with the eyes of a painter.

SPRING, 1573
Giuseppe Arcimboldo, Italian (1527–93), oil on canvas, 29 ⅞" x 25 ¼"

Giuseppe Arcimboldo lived during the Renaissance, when the cultural values of ancient Greece were reborn in a flowering of the arts, literature, and science. Arcimboldo took a cosmic view of the universe, originally expressed by the Greek philosopher Plato in the fifth century B.C. Arcimboldo believed that all living things—humans, plants, and animals—were perfectly balanced in a natural scheme that runs like clockwork.

Arcimboldo created a series of allegorical paintings of the four seasons in a unique style. He symbolized spring as the sunlight and air that bring new growth after winter in this portraitlike image formed of interlocking flowers and leaves.

Using a technique called trompe l'oeil, Arcimboldo fools the eye into believing that these flowers, which are painted on a flat surface, are three-dimensional.

Arcimboldo's careful observation and fine brushwork give these flowers a lifelike presence, as seen in this detail.

Arcimboldo also tricks the viewer into seeing the blossoms as a young woman's face and clothing. He painted her skin as a field of pale flowers, her nose as a lily bud, and her dress as an exuberant display of leaves. The complexity of the blossom and leaf patterns expresses Arcimboldo's belief in the almost mechanical precision of nature.

Although this painting was created more than three hundred years ago, the flowers seem as fresh as spring itself because Arcimboldo used the best and costliest of pigments, including kermes red made from Far Eastern insects and paint made of gold. He worked with fine brushes to achieve the delicate tracery that makes each flower stand out as a unique specimen.

Arcimboldo's talent, imagination, and wit were appreciated by two generations of Holy Roman emperors. For twenty-five years, Arcimboldo was the official court painter to Maximilian II and his son, Rudolph II.

A YOUNG DAUGHTER OF THE PICTS, about 1585
Jacques Le Moyne de Morgues, French (c. 1533–88)
Watercolor and gouache on vellum, 10 ⅛" x 7 ¼"

*E*arly explorers of the New World wrote about the beauty and variety of exotic flowers that flourished there. The news inspired a French botanical painter named Jacques Le Moyne de Morgues to make the long and dangerous journey by ship to the Floridas in 1564. Le Morgues kept a journal of his impressions of the Native Americans, whose way of life was intimately connected with the natural world. About twenty years later, while living in England, de Morgues evoked his American experience in this painting.

Le Morgues was fascinated by an early British tribe called the Picts, who painted their bodies for war. He portrayed a Pictish woman warrior to demonstrate that the British, like the Americans, had an ancient tribal history. Le Morgues personified the young woman as Flora, goddess of flowers. He adorned her body with glorious blossoms, many of which had recently been brought to Europe from the New World.

Le Morgues used both *transparent watercolor* and an *opaque* paint called *gouache*. First he laid out the *composition* with pencil. Using transparent watercolor, Le Morgues painted the clouds and the hills, leaving white paper uncovered for the fort. He created Flora's delicate skin tones with transparent peach and modeled the contours of her figure with golden shading. Over this, Le Morgues formed a tapestry of flowers in gouache, detailed with the accuracy of a botanical study. Delicate wildflowers at her feet, painted with transparent colors, visually connect Flora with her earthly domain.

Although little is known about Le Morgues's personal life, the written records of his journeys from France to North America and to the British Isles show that he embraced the spirit of the age of exploration.

Martin Johnson Heade (1819–1904) captured an orchid's regal contours in an oil painting based on drawings he made during an expedition to South America in the 1860s.

11

FLOWERS, ANIMALS, AND INSECTS, about 1670
Abraham Mignon, Dutch (1640–79), oil on canvas, 28 ¾" x 23 ⅝"

*F*lower painting became a major art form during the seventeenth century in the Netherlands. When Spain's Catholic influence there subsided after the defeat of the Spanish Armada in 1588, painters who had previously created religious art for churches searched for new patrons. During this time, there emerged an affluent middle class of bankers and merchants who eagerly collected nature scenes to decorate their homes. Abraham Mignon, about whom little is known except that he was a *still life* specialist, created this woodland view of nature in microcosm.

In a sheltered glade, a clump of wildflowers symbolizing purity almost conceals a snake poised to attack a field mouse. The forest teems with animals and with plants in various stages of growth and decay.

In this detail we see that Abraham Mignon contrasted the innocent beauty of an oxeye daisy with the deadly menace of a snake poised to strike.

Mignon created a lighting scheme that dramatizes this moment in nature's eternal cycle. Strong sunlight creeps in from the left, *silhouetting* a clump of mushrooms that frames the scene. By placing the light source in the *foreground,* Mignon darkened the *background* with *shadows* that focus attention on the drama about to unfold.

To achieve the almost microscopic *detail* in this picture, Mignon gradually built up the painting in thin layers that enabled him to work slowly and carefully. First he blocked out the entire scene in golden umber. He blended blue with green to form the foliage in cool silvery hues that *contrast* with the warm umber *tones* that shine through the painting. With fine brushes he precisely rendered the flowers, insects, and animals.

Mignon's deep understanding of nature makes this painting a masterpiece of artistic vision and *design* rather than a scientifically accurate study.

EGRET AND MALLOW PLANTS, date unknown
Yamamoto Baiitsu, Japanese (1783–1856), ink and colors on silk, 73" x 21½"

Yamamoto Baiitsu lived during a time when Japanese merchants had become wealthier than the imperial warlords who then governed. The middle classes were banned from political life, so they built lavish homes to express their status. To show that they were not merely rich but also cultivated, they *commissioned* artists to create beautiful paintings on silk scrolls.

In this landscape with flowers, Baiitsu depicts the tremendous variety of natural forms he observed at the edge of a marsh. He created a wide range of autumnal hues by diluting a brown-toned *ink*, called sumi, with water for the palest shades and painting with a nearly dry brush to make the dark tones. Baiitsu first blocked out the mallow flowers in *opaque* white paint that covers the golden silk background. With a fine brush he then shaped the delicate pink blossoms, letting some white show through to separate the petals from each other.

Baiitsu balanced the large forms of the snowy white egret and the cliff with grasses and foliage painted in finely patterned brushstrokes. The horizontal shapes of the pond, a sweeping arc of sea grass, and the bird's long bill complement strong vertical elements in the bird's pencil-thin leg, the tall branch of mallow, and the vertical format of the scroll itself.

Baiitsu achieved his great artistry through a lifetime spent in the quiet contemplation of nature. In this painting he expresses the traditional Japanese respect for all living things, even the tiniest blade of grass.

This close-up reveals Baiitsu's skill in creating a variety of shades and textures from three hues: pink, white, and brownish black.

SPRING BOUQUET, 1866
Pierre-Auguste Renoir, French (1841–1919), oil on canvas, 41¾" x 32"

*P*ierre-Auguste Renoir began his painting career as a commercial artist who decorated expensive porcelain vases, but he soon realized that his talent was being limited. In 1862, Renoir enrolled in the prestigious Ecole Impériale et Spéciale des Beaux-Arts in Paris, France. His good friend and fellow student Jules Le Coeur introduced Renoir to his brother Charles, a prominent architect who *commissioned* this painting.

In this *still life*, Renoir evokes not only the mood but also the sensation of looking at a glorious bouquet of flowers. He had observed that *shadows* were never black in hazy outdoor light. Instead they take on the colors of nearby objects. The white flowers in this bouquet, like little reflectors, cast light blue shadows that mirror the color of the sky. Renoir exaggerated this effect to create a luminous bouquet of flowers that seems to be lighted from within.

Renoir created a feast of *textures* by using thin and thick layers of paint. He modeled the ruffled petals of the peonies with rose and mauve hues delicately worked into wet white paint diluted with turpentine. For the lilacs, Renoir painted a blur of *transparent* blue over the green tone of the leaves. He then formed a multitude of tiny lavender blossoms with touches of *opaque* paint. Renoir produced a feeling of depth in the bouquet through his use of cool green hues in the foliage, which appear more distant than the warm yellows and whites in the flowers.

Using large brushes and thickly applied patches of yellow, blue, and green, Renoir created the effect of dappled sunlight around the flowers. By contrast, the boldly textured surface of the *background* heightens the viewer's awareness of the fragile delicacy of the spring bouquet.

PINKS AND CLEMATIS IN A CRYSTAL VASE, 1882
Edouard Manet, French (1832–83), oil on canvas, 22" x 13¾"

In 1882 an illness that would soon end his life forced Edouard Manet to move to the country for rest. His Parisian friends made frequent visits and brought bouquets of flowers. Able to work for only short periods of time, Manet created a series of intimate flower paintings. He captured the beauty of these cut flowers with the same attention that he had previously given to *portraits* of lovely women.

Manet's gift for observation is demonstrated in this picture, for there is not a hint of indecision or struggle in the work. He formed the clematis with broad areas of *opaque* violet touched with a deeper shade that defines the fragile petals. Manet blended shades of pink and red paint to depict the carnationlike pinks, adding touches of white that define their multipetal forms. Manet shaped the leaves in masses of bluish green and used the wooden end of a brush to scratch *lines* on the wet paint to depict the veins of the leaves.

The vase is a triumph of vision and *design*. Manet conveyed the weight and clarity of crystal with bold deliberate strokes of *transparent* gray and cerulean blue. With tones of golden copper and white on the glass and water, he created prismlike reflections that distort the stems. As in many of his *portraits*, Manet painted a plain *background* to focus attention on the flowers. By adding violet to the gray hue, he created a vibrant *tone* that brings the delicate clematis to life.

This exquisite painting seems like a gift from Manet to all of the friends who gave him bouquets of fresh flowers.

A cascade of roses set against a dark background complements this woman's delicate beauty in a portrait by William Thorne (1863–1956).

19

WILD ROSES AND IRISES, 1887
John La Farge, American (1835–1910), watercolor on paper, 12⅝" x 10⅛"

John La Farge reached his artistic maturity during America's Gilded Age in the late nineteenth century. This was a time when men who had made fortunes building railroads and steel mills used their wealth to establish universities and public libraries. They hired the best architects to design new buildings and the best artists to decorate them. In 1876, La Farge, already an acclaimed painter, became one of the most sought after designers of murals and stained glass windows.

For his decorative projects, La Farge created small-scale *watercolor* studies to show his clients how the final designs would appear. In the 1870s he began a series of watercolor flower paintings as finished works of art. In this picture of irises and roses, La Farge expressed his enjoyment of nature and of the watercolor medium itself.

By studying Japanese art, La Farge learned a new way of depicting objects in space. He formed a flat *background* of foliage to focus attention on the flowers. By abruptly cutting off the irises at the edge of the paper, he conveys its nearness to the viewer and distance from the greenery in the background.

Katsushika Hokusai (1760–1849) carefully designed the spaces between the irises and the leaves to represent air, which is as much a part of nature as are plants and animals.

La Farge combined *transparent* and *opaque* watercolor paint to express the delicacy of the blossoms and powerful forms of the stems. He blended transparent blue and indigo hues on wet paper to shape the complex petals. Leaving areas of white paper unpainted, La Farge suggested sunlight shining through the delicate flowers.

La Farge's watercolor paintings were in great demand during his lifetime. On more than one occasion, he paid off his debts through the exhibition and sale of these superb nature studies.

20

231

SUNFLOWERS, 1889
Vincent van Gogh, Dutch (1853–90), oil on canvas, 37 ⅜" x 28 ¾"

Vincent van Gogh moved from Holland to Paris, France, in 1884. After two years, van Gogh felt depleted by the late nights spent in cafés, drinking and talking with other painters. He moved to Arles, in the south of France, where he could paint outdoors in the brilliant sunshine.

Landscape painting was van Gogh's primary interest. But when the weather was bad he created *still-life* paintings in his studio. This was an ideal way for van Gogh to study the interaction of colors. In this painting of sunflowers, he studied the way bright shades of yellow appear to change when placed next to each other. Van Gogh knew that the evenly balanced values of the *background* and flowers would make all of the brilliant yellows appear to be less intense than they actually are, thereby creating a tranquil effect.

Van Gogh maintained the clarity of his colors by avoiding the use of shading. He gave three-dimensional form to the flowers and vase through expressive *lines* and *textures*. Van Gogh shaped the flowers in linear strokes of yellow against ocher, separating the spiky petals from their centers. He conveyed the round form of the seed heads with thickly textured yellow paint dotted into the orange while it was still wet. An expressive outline and patches of orange-yellow make the vase appear three-dimensional.

During van Gogh's 444-day visit to Arles he made two hundred paintings and more than one hundred *drawings*. He also wrote two hundred letters that tell of his passionate feelings about art and life.

Van Gogh explored the powerful jagged forms of dried sunflowers in this oil painting.

BLUE LILY, about 1908
Piet Mondrian, Dutch (1872–1944), graphite and watercolor on paper,
10½" x 6⅞"

*P*iet Mondrian is famous for his *abstract* paintings: precisely designed grids in black and white and vibrant primary colors. Before he began to make abstract paintings in 1914, however, Mondrian found inspiration in nature. He grew up in the Netherlands and shared the Dutch passion for flowers. Mondrian's close-up paintings of single flowers express both joy and sadness: a blossom picked at its most glorious moment that quickly wilts.

Before he painted this picture, Mondrian first made careful *drawings* to study a freshly cut lily's intricate construction and to observe the way it changed after he put it in water. The wonder of this painting is the simplicity with which he captured the red markings that bled as the petals began to wither.

Mondrian achieved a *transparent* effect with *watercolor* thinly diluted to create luminous yellows, blues, and purples. He first sketched out the *composition* exactly as he wanted to see the flower on the page. Mondrian then wet the paper thoroughly and spread a tint of golden yellow over the *background*, brushing the color up to the outline of the flower and stem. While the paper was still damp, he painted the

lily a pale, watery blue, leaving areas of white paper uncovered to convey the effect of light gleaming through the blossom. Dots of vermilion applied to the moist paper spread to form the petals' bleeding marks.

After he was internationally acclaimed for his geometric abstractions, Mondrian insisted that he hated nature. However, he secretly continued to create floral paintings that express his poetic fascination with dying flowers.

Georges Braque (1892–1963) used an inky black border to emphasize the geometric shapes in the background of this color etching.

P. MONDRIAAN

25

PORTRAIT OF MÄDA PRIMAVESI, about 1912–13
Gustav Klimt, Austrian (1862–1918), oil on canvas, 59" x 43 ½"

Gustav Klimt began his professional career while he was still a student at the School of Applied Arts in Vienna, Austria. Klimt, his brother Ernst, and a fellow student were selected by an instructor to help produce stained glass windows for a new church. The three young artists then opened a workshop in which they created murals and decorations for public buildings. As he became well known Klimt attracted a circle of affluent *patrons* including Otto Primavesi, who *commissioned* this *portrait* of his daughter Mäda.

Klimt depicted the lovely ten-year-old girl in a floral fairyland. He created a puzzling space that could be a landscape or a living room. The ground might be viewed as a garden path or a flower-patterned carpet. Klimt chose a point of view from below that gives Mäda monumental scale. He creates a dreamlike mood through the *contrast* between her realistically painted figure and the more *abstractly* painted *background*.

Salvador Dalí (1904–1989) cast large shadows of the flowers and butterflies against the rocks, making the woman seated on the cliff seem small and distant by comparison.

Klimt focuses attention on his young subject through the combination of two very different painting techniques. Using fine brushes, he shaped Mäda's features with delicate shading; for the floral background, Klimt used large brushes and thick swirls of paint that dance across the *canvas*. Mäda's dress gleams with bold brushstrokes of yellow, blue, and mauve that Klimt painted into a wet layer of white paint. He embellished the dress with a *design* that echoes the flowers on the ground and emphasizes the patterned *composition*.

Gustav Klimt's commitment to both the fine and the decorative arts was recognized by his fellow artists who elected him president of the Austrian Artists' Union in 1912, around the time that he created this painting.

BLUE WATER LILIES, about 1916–19
Claude Monet, French (1840–1926), oil on canvas, 78" x 78 ¾"

In 1883, Claude Monet moved to Giverny, France. There he constructed a water lily pond that gradually became the main subject of his work. Monet wrote to a friend: "I'm absorbed in work. These landscapes showing water and reflections have become an obsession .... I want to represent what I experience."

In this painting, Monet conveyed the way he saw the surface of the pond transformed by sunlight. The willow branches at the top and their reflections below frame the picture with darkly *contrasting* strands of green, umber, and black. At the edges, Monet left areas of the *canvas* blank to suggest beams of light filtering through the trees. He painted areas of bright cerulean blue over deep blue-violet to depict reflections of the sky on the water. The thickly textured paint takes on the lively quality of the water's rippled surface as seen at close range.

Because aquatic flowers close their petals at dusk, Monet painted rapidly to capture the mood of late afternoon *shadows* on the water. He blended white into the blue-violet color of the water to suggest mist in the *background*. Monet expressed the delicacy of the flowers with translucent white paint, adding thick white *highlights* built up from the canvas.

In the hundreds of water lily paintings and studies that Monet worked on between 1916 and 1926, he created an emotional way of painting that was never imitated during his lifetime. In this series the act of painting and the richly textured paint surface are Monet's major themes, whereas the lily pond is a secondary theme by comparison.

NIGHT FLOWERS, 1918
Paul Klee, German (1879–1940), watercolor on paper, 7" x 6 ⁷⁄₁₆"

*A*s a child Paul Klee was fascinated with flowers and grew daisies in his own miniature garden. At ten, Klee created a series of sketchbooks dedicated to flowers: accurate botanical studies as well as *drawings* of imaginary specimens. As he grew up Klee realized that through the close study of nature he could explore the spiritual side of life.

In this imaginary scene, Klee deliberately created simplified, almost primitive, images of flowers, trees, and ferns to depict a place that might well be the Garden of Eden. For Klee, the ordinary daisy, which often flourishes in bad soil, symbolized the tenacity of the plant kingdom. With its simple symmetrical arrangement of white petals around a yellow center, the daisy symbolizes the sun—the source of life for plants.

Klee did not depict a naturalistic space using the technique of *perspective*. Instead, he created the feeling of depth through the use of color. Because intense warm colors such as red appear to be closer to the viewer than pale cool colors such as blue, Klee created the effect of great distance between the red tower in the *foreground* and the pale blue fir tree in the *background*. In *contrast* to the pink cloudlike forms that frame the scene on two sides, the soft blue background seems as far away as a distant galaxy.

Small and large evergreen trees and ferns floating through the landscape convey nature's continuous cycle of birth, growth, death, and rebirth. The red observation tower suggests a human presence in Klee's twilight garden.

Using translucent white paint, Klee created the magic of moonlight shining through daisy petals.

WHITE SWEET PEAS, 1926
Georgia O'Keeffe, American (1887–1986), pastel on paper, 25" x 19"

In the 1920s, Georgia O'Keeffe spent her winters in New York City. Looking out from her twenty-eighth-floor studio she painted pictures of skyscrapers under construction. Although O'Keeffe admired these huge modern buildings, she felt cut off from nature, so she began to paint flowers. O'Keeffe wrote: "When you take a flower into your hands and really look at it, it's your world for the moment. I want to give that world to someone else." In this painting of sweet peas, O'Keeffe chose a close-up point of view to engulf the viewer in the mysterious world of flowers.

The freshness and clarity of O'Keeffe's colors is a result of her approach to the craft of painting. In her memory O'Keeffe nurtured earlier observations of living flowers. After she had formed a clear mental image of the shapes, *textures*, and colors, she then began to paint. O'Keeffe worked without hesitation, never changing her mind and never making corrections that might have resulted in muddy colors.

O'Keefe painted this picture using *pastels*, sticks of soft colored chalk. Starting with white, the brightest color in her *palette*, she shaped the petals by blending in bright, or high-key, hues of turquoise and yellow. For the shading she applied a cool mauve color. To achieve subtle gradations from white to mauve, as seen on the large flower at the left, she used a dry paintbrush to blend the velvety tones.

The sweet peas in this picture are enlarged to about seventeen times their actual size. The lush, precisely formed petals emerging from a limitless *background* suggest that we can become one with the mysterious world of nature.

GERANIUM, about 1926
Charles Sheeler, American (1883–1965), oil on canvas, 32" x 26"

Charles Sheeler was trained as an artist and later worked as a commercial photographer in order to support his family. He was fascinated by the ways in which a photograph can change the look of ordinary objects. Sheeler brought both the reality and the illusions of photography to his paintings.

At first glance this painting seems to be a straightforward view of an ordinary flower. Sheeler dramatically backlighted the plant and positioned it against a stark *background* to focus attention on the single red flower. He cropped the picture, abruptly cutting off the image at the edge to spotlight the subject. A closer look, however, reveals Sheeler's subtle and sophisticated *composition.*

Sheeler altered our perception of space in this scene by using several points of view. We see the geranium straight on, whereas the table and chair are depicted from high above. Sheeler tilted the table at a steep angle that projects the plant forward in space. As the result of these distortions of *perspective,* we seem to be moving through the space depicted in the painting.

Sheeler worked with two distinct painting techniques. He used fine brushes to carefully render the geranium and the furnishings. We sense the cool smooth surface of the china dish, crisply defined with blue *shadows* and white *highlights.* For the background, however, he painted expressive *textures* with big brushes, creating a soft-focus impression of light.

Although the objects in this *still life* are motionless, the changing perspective and varying techniques convey a feeling of movement, which makes us feel that we are viewing the scene at different moments in time.

Joseph Stella (1877–1946) drew this picture with a fine rod called silverpoint, which deposits metal particles on paper. Over time the silver particles tarnish, forming rich black lines.

THE PURPLE ROBE, 1937
Henri Matisse, French (1869–1954), oil on canvas, 28 ¾" x 23 ¾"

In the mid-1930s, economic depression and the threat of another war in Europe made Henri Matisse feel anxious. He moved back to Paris from the south of France, where he had begun to feel isolated from the art world. Matisse filled his new studio with flowers, decorative wall hangings, and exotic birds that reminded him of the enchanted surroundings he had enjoyed on a visit to Tahiti.

For Matisse, the subject of a picture (in this case, flowers and a woman) and the *background* were one. Through the careful balance of colors, *lines*, and forms, Matisse created a joyous expression. He echoed the rhythmical lines of the anemone stems in the fluted vase, in the flowing stripes of the purple robe, and in the wavy white lines decorating the curtain. Matisse patterned the *designs* on the table and the woman's skirt after floral shapes. The curved lines and patterns throughout the painting are balanced by straight lines on the striped carpet and wallpaper and on the tiled floor.

Although Matisse used bright shades of red and yellow in the flowers and in the striped background, he evokes a tranquil mood through the large areas of clear blue-green that balance the brilliant hues. He progressively lightened this color by adding white to the woman's skirt and the curtain behind her to create a feeling of distance from the *foreground* to the background. With a strip of black, Matisse defined the edges of the room and gave a feeling of depth to the flatly painted picture.

Matisse appreciated life's sensuous pleasures. In this intimate interior scene he expressed the pleasure that luxury and beauty gave him.

Henri Matisse varied the thickness of the lines in this linoleum cut, creating many different shades of white.

THE FLOWER VENDOR, 1941
Diego Rivera, Mexican (1886–1957), oil on canvas, 48" x 48"

In 1907, Diego Rivera moved from Mexico to Europe to study painting. For fourteen years the gifted young artist absorbed the influence of modern painting as it was being redefined by Pablo Picasso and Joan Miró. Although Rivera's work attracted attention, it was an imitation rather than a true expression of his identity as an artist.

Only when he returned to his own country did Rivera create a powerful, distinctive style. He immersed himself in Mexico's pre-Columbian art and culture, which had flourished until the fifteenth century. After Spanish conquistadores pillaged the country and subjugated the native people, the Aztec civilization died out.

In this painting of an Aztec woman with flowers, Rivera created an image that has the impact of an ancient stone carving. Using bold, simplified forms, he emphasized the woman's stoic grace as she gently places an enormous mass of calla lilies on the ground. Rivera enlarged the scale of the flowers to fill the square *canvas* almost to the edges. The dark *background* creates a frame that draws attention to the enormous lilies, which Rivera painted in delicate tints of green, yellow, and white.

Rivera created a feeling of spatial depth through the dynamic shapes of the flowers. The petals and stems are shown head on at the center of the picture. Closer to the edges, the petals turn in profile and the stems curve rhythmically toward the distance.

Rivera demonstrates his kinship with folk artists of earlier times by signing his name on a little note card, a tradition in Mexican folk painting.

Rivera's bold watercolor brush marks become masses of marigolds, flowers traditionally displayed during the Aztec Day of the Dead celebration.

THE FLOWER BARGE, 1954
André Bauchant, French (1873–1958), oil on canvas, 28 ¼" x 38 ½"

*A*ndré Bauchant left school at age fourteen to work in his father's nursery garden. Although his formal education was brief, Bauchant continued to read history and mythology for enjoyment. Later, when he was in the army, Bauchant recalled these stories of great events and legendary feats to escape the boredom of military life. When he was released from service in 1920, Bauchant began painting pictures inspired by the mythological scenes that had become larger than life in his mind.

Bauchant created distortions of *scale* to great effect in his picture of a barge overflowing with flowers. The buildings, trees, and the boat itself are in proportion to the vine-covered wall and bouquets in the *foreground*. The enormous blossoms in the barge are out of proportion with the boat itself. However, we can also view the flower barge as a bouquet that is in perfect proportion to the wall and the two bouquets in the foreground. Either way we read this painting, Bauchant's love of flowers is clearly expressed.

Bauchant wanted to convey his visions exactly as he had imagined them, so he depicted everything in minute detail. The little house in the distance is rendered with the same precision as the flowers in the foreground. He maintained the intensity of his colors throughout, rather than softening the hues in the *background*, which is a method often used by painters to convey depth. Like many folk artists, Bauchant developed a style based on his imagination rather than on conventional ideas about painting.

Although Bauchant was a self-taught painter, he worked with assurance from the beginning. Bauchant's sophisticated style immediately brought him success through the patronage of the great French architect Le Corbusier.

Like a sentinel standing guard, an exuberant little bouquet heralds the arrival of Bauchant's fabulous flower barge.

40

THE WRESTLERS' TOMB, 1960
René Magritte, Belgian (1898–1967), oil on canvas, 38" x 51"

René Magritte trusted his dreams to reveal the hidden meaning of ordinary objects. Magritte called himself a painter, not an artist, for he was not interested in depicting beautiful things. His was a world of ideas.

When faced with the problem of how to convey the essence of a rose, Magritte thought about the qualities that give that flower a powerful presence. He dramatically enlarged this rose to convey the idea of its aroma taking over a room. What we cannot tell is whether he has depicted a large rose in a small room or a true-to-*scale* rose in a miniature room. By creating a picture that is also a puzzle, Magritte urges us to think in unconventional ways.

Magritte established that this is not a work of art but a picture of an idea through a precise, super-realistic, painting style. He referred to an advertising photograph to reproduce the rose's perfectly formed petals. With fine brushes, Magritte carefully blended shades of bright red paint, leaving neither brush marks nor *textures* that might reveal the touch of an artist's hand on the surface of the *canvas*. He placed the rose in an ordinary room, rendered in toned-down shades of reddish brown that set off the brilliant flower. Although there is a window that admits natural light, Magritte beamed harsh artificial light from an unseen source in front of the painting, forming dark *shadows* that almost project the flower out of the picture.

Magritte observed that most people have predictable ways of looking at life, whereas he saw that reality offers many possibilities. In this unsettling picture, Magritte suggests that a rose can have more than one kind of presence.

CAMELLIAS, 1991
Robert Kushner, American (born 1949), oil and gold leaf on canvas, 72" x 36"

*A*s a child in southern California, Robert Kushner played in a backyard luxuriant with roses and hibiscus. One of his earliest memories was of escaping to the garden next door to smell the sultry perfume of the camellias. The sheer beauty of the flowers of his childhood later inspired Kushner in his paintings.

His painting *Camellias* not only celebrates the romantic beauty of that flower but also honors the traditions of eighteenth-century Japanese painting. Early Japanese artists created *backgrounds* of *gold leaf* to reflect light and create a mood of extravagance and splendor. Kushner adopted traditional materials and methods of Japanese painting to create a personal interpretation of a timeless art.

Kushner first made a series of *drawings* to study the camellias and plan the *composition*—the layout of flowers on a background grid of square and rectangular color blocks.

Like Japanese painters, Kushner worked with the *canvas* flat on the floor in order to control the flow of wet paint and avoid paint drips. Using brushes with long flexible bristles, Kushner formed the rhythmical outlines of flowers and leaves. He then created the background, varying the textures from a flat, smooth area of ultramarine to a thick application of cerulean blue. After the paint was dry he placed squares of gold leaf over half of the background. The gleaming gold squares form a grid pattern in tune with the two square canvases that make up this large painting.

Robert Kushner's earliest ambition was to become a horticulturist. Today he balances his work as a painter with the pleasure of growing flowers for his own and his family's enjoyment.

Sharp details in the monarch butterfly, in contrast to the blurred roses in the background, emphasize the super-realistic style of contemporary artist Audrey Flack (born 1931).

Glossary and Index

46

OIL PAINT: Pigment is combined with an oil vehicle (usually linseed or poppy oil). The medium chosen by most artists is linseed oil. The solvent is turpentine. Oil paint is never mixed with water. Oils dry slowly, enabling the artist to work on a painting for a long time. Some painters add other materials, such as pumice powder or marble dust, to produce thick layers of color. Oil paint has been used since the fifteenth century. Until the early nineteenth century, artists or their assistants ground the pigment and combined the ingredients of paint in their studios. When the flexible tin tube (like a toothpaste tube) was invented in 1840, paint made by art suppliers became available.

TEMPERA: Pigment is combined with a water-based vehicle. The paint is combined with raw egg yolk to "temper" it into a mayonnaiselike consistency usable with a brush. The solvent for tempera is water. Tempera was used by the ancient Greeks and was the favorite medium of painters in medieval Europe. It is now available in tubes, ready to use. The painter supplies the egg yolk.

WATERCOLOR: Pigment is combined with gum arabic, a water-based vehicle. Water is both the medium and the solvent. Watercolor paint now comes ready to use in tubes (moist) or in cakes (dry). Watercolor paint is thinned with water, and areas of paper are often left uncovered to produce highlights.

Gouache is an opaque form of watercolor, which is also called tempera or body color.

Watercolor paint was first used 37,000 years ago by cave dwellers who created the first wall paintings.

PASTEL, 30: (1) A soft crayon made of powdered pigment, chalk, and water mixed with a small amount of gum to form a stick. (2) A painting made with this type of crayon.

PATRON, 24: An individual, or organization, that supports the arts or an individual artist.

PERSPECTIVE, 28, 32: Perspective is a method of representing people, places, and things in a painting or drawing to make them appear solid or three-dimensional rather than flat. Six basic rules of perspective are used in Western art.

1. People in a painting appear larger when near and gradually become smaller as they get farther away.
2. People in the foreground overlap people or objects behind them.
3. People become closer together as they get farther away.
4. People in the distance are closer to the top of the picture than those in the foreground.
5. Colors are brighter and shadows are stronger in the foreground. Colors and shadows are paler and softer in the background. This technique is often called *atmospheric perspective*.
6. Lines that in real life are parallel (such as the line of a ceiling and the line of a floor) are drawn at an angle, and the lines meet at the *horizon line*, which represents the eye level of the artist and the viewer.

In addition, a special technique of perspective, called *foreshortening*, is used to compensate for distortion in figures and objects painted on a flat surface. For example, an artist will paint the hand of an outstretched arm larger than it is in proportion to the arm, which becomes smaller as it recedes toward the shoulder. This correction, necessary in a picture using perspective, is automatically made by the human eye observing a scene in life. *Foreshortening* refers to the representation of figures or objects, whereas *perspective* refers to the representation of a scene or a space.

Painters have used these methods to depict objects in space since the fifteenth century. However, many twentieth-century artists choose not to use perspective. An artist might emphasize colors, lines, or shapes to express an idea instead of showing people or objects in a realistic space.

Credits

Frontispiece

THE WHITE HERON, 1918–20
Joseph Stella, American (1877–1964)
Oil on canvas, 48 ⅛" x 29 ⅛"
Yale University Art Gallery, New Haven, Connecticut 1941.691

Page

9 *SPRING*, 1573
Giuseppe Arcimboldo, Italian
Musée de Louvre © Photo R.M.N.

10 *STILL LIFE WITH CATTELAYA, TWO HUMMINGBIRDS, AND BEETLE*,
Martin Johnson Heade, American
Oil on canvas, 14 ¼" x 22 ¼" (detail)
Private Collection

11 *A YOUNG DAUGHTER OF THE PICTS*, c.1585
Jacques Le Moyne de Morgues, French
Yale Center for British Art, New Haven, Connecticut
Paul Mellon Collection

13 *FLOWERS, ANIMALS, AND INSECTS*, c. 1670
Abraham Mignon, Dutch
Musées Royaux des Beaux–Arts de Belgique, Brussels

15 *EGRET AND MALLOW PLANTS*, Edo Period, date unknown
Yamamoto Baiitsu, Japanese
Courtesy Dr. & Mrs. Kurt Gitter, New Orleans

17 *SPRING BOUQUET*, 1866
Pierre–Auguste Renoir, French
Fogg Art Museum, Cambridge, Massachusetts
Harvard University Art Museums
Bequest of Grenville L. Winthrop

18 *WOMAN IN KIMONO*, 1892, (detail)
William Thorn, American (1863–1956)
Oil on canvas, 32 ¾" x 11 ½"
Courtesy ACA Gallery, New York

19 *PINKS AND CLEMATIS IN A CRYSTAL VASE*, 1882
Edouard Manet, French
Musée D'Orsay © Photo R.M.N.

20 *IRISES*, c.1822
Katsushika Hokusai, Japanese (1760–1849)
Print 9 ¾" x 14 ³⁄₁₆"
The Metropolitan Museum of Art, New York
Frederick Charles Hewitt Bequest Fund, 1912

21 *WILD ROSES AND IRISES*, 1887
John La Farge, American
The Metropolitan Museum of Art, New York
Gift of Priscilla A.B. Henderson in memory of her grandfather, Russell St. Sturgis,
a founder of the Metropolitan Museum

22 *SUNFLOWERS*, 1887
Vincent van Gogh, Dutch
Oil on canvas, 17" x 24"
The Metropolitan Museum of Art, New York
Rogers Fund, 1949

23 *SUNFLOWERS*, 1889
Vincent van Gogh, Dutch
The Metropolitan Museum of Art, New York
Rogers Fund, 1949. (49.41.)

25 *BLUE LILY*, c. 1908
Piet Mondrian, Dutch
Courtesy Sidney Janis Gallery, New York

26 *THE LORELEI*, 1948
Salvador Dali, Spanish
Watercolor on paper
Courtesy Mrs. Albert D. Lasker

27 *PORTRAIT OF MÄDA PRIMAVESI*, c. 1912–13
Gustav Klimt, Austrian
The Metropolitan Museum of Art, New York
Gift of Andre and Clara Mertens, in memory of her mother Jenny Pulitzer Steiner,
1964. (64.148.)

29 *BLUE WATER LILLIES*, c. 1916–19
Claude Monet, French
Musée D'Orsay © Photo R.M.N. SPADEM

31 *NIGHT FLOWERS*, 1918
Paul Klee, German
Museum Folkwang, Essen

33 *WHITE SWEET PEAS*, 1926
Georgia O'Keeffe, American
Private Collection

34 *YELLOW LOTUS*, 1920
Joseph Stella, American (1877–1946)
Silverpoint and crayon on paper, 7 ⅞" x 10 ⅝"
Collection of Mr. and Mrs. Eric P. Widing
Courtesy Richard York Gallery, New York

35 *GERANIUM*, c. 1926
Charles Sheeler, American
Collection of Whitney Museum of American Art, New York
Gift of Gertrude Vanderbilt Whitney 31.343.

36 *THE BASKET OF FLOWERS*, 1917
Georges Braque, French
Courtesy Hubert Gallery, New York

36 *BASKET OF BEGONIAS*, 1938
Henri Matisse, French
Courtesy Isselbacher Gallery, New York

37 *PURPLE ROBE AND ANEMONES*, 1937
Henri Matisse, French
The Baltimore Museum of Art: The Cone Collection, formed by Dr. Claribel Cone
and Miss Etta Cone of Baltimore, Maryland, (BMA 1950.261.)

38 *WOMAN WITH MARIGOLDS*, 1954
Diego Rivera, Mexican
Watercolor on paper, 15 ¼" x 11"
Courtesy Mary–Anne Martin/Fine Art, New York

39 *THE FLOWER VENDOR*, 1941
Diego Rivera, Mexican
Norton Simon Museum, Pasadena, California
(P. 1980.2.3.) Gift of Mr. Cary Grant, 1980

41 *THE FLOWER BOAT*, 1941
André Bauchant, French
Courtesy Mrs. Albert D. Lasker

43 *THE WRESTLER'S TOMB*, 1960
René Magritte, Belgian
© 1993 C. Herscovici / ARS, NY
Photo courtesy Mr. Harry Torczyner

44 *MONARCH AND ROSE*, 1980
Audrey Flack, American
Acrylic on paper 15" x 21 ½"
Courtesy Louis K. Meisel Gallery, New York, Photo: Steve Lopez

45 *CAMELLIAS*, 1991
Robert Kushner, American
Courtesy Midtown Payson Gallery, New York